P9-DCP-193

Ellie's Long Walk

The True Story of Two Friends on the Appalachian Trail

Written by **Pam Flowers**

Illustrations by **Bill Farnsworth**

A&A JOHNSTON PRESS™

*E*llie raced to the side of the puppy pen to see who was coming. When she saw Pam, Ellie reached up with her tiny front paws as if to say,

"Pick me! Pick ME!"

There were seven little puppies. All needed a home.

Ellie was black with a white blaze on her chest. When Ellie and Pam looked at each other, the puppy sat right down, lowered her head, and pulled her ears back, showing good dog manners.

Pam smiled and scooped Ellie into her arms. "I'll adopt this one. She behaves and will make a nice friend."

Ellie moved into a big, round pen next to Pam's desk so they could be together all day. The puppy wagged her tail as she sniffed every inch of her new home.

"I see you like to explore new places, Ellie" Pam said. "Me, too! You and I are going to make a fine team."

When Ellie was about six months old, Pam began making plans to hike the Appalachian Trail. The Trail is more than 2,000 miles long, stretching from Maine to Georgia. Pam would have to walk many long hours every day for six months to hike the whole thing. She wanted company but wondered if Ellie was too young for such a difficult journey.

The only way to find out was to start training. For the next two months Pam and Ellie walked three hours every day. Ellie didn't mind in the least. She loved going for long walks with Pam.

"Maybe you *can* hike the Trail," Pam said. But there was still something else young Ellie needed to learn.

On the Appalachian Trail they would both carry packs on their backs. Pam would carry a tent, sleeping bag, food, and maps. Ellie would carry her food, a bowl, and her toenail clippers.

Pack training started right away. When Pam first strapped Ellie's pack on her, the puppy jumped straight up, spun around, and tried to shake it off.

Pam laughed as she straightened the pack. "Don't worry, you'll get used to it."

That first day, they wore empty packs.

Each day Pam added small weights. The packs got heavier and heavier. After four months, Pam and Ellie could carry fully loaded packs and walk six miles without getting tired.

They were ready to begin their journey.

$\mathcal{F}$inally, the big day arrived.

It was August, Ellie was thirteen months old, and Pam had just driven them all the way from Alaska to Maine to start their hike. At the head of the Trail, Ellie barked and bounced up and down. She was as excited as Pam to get started.

"Ready to go for a REEEAALLY long walk?" Pam asked.

Ellie stood with her mouth open and her tongue hanging out in a big doggie smile as if to say,

"You bet!"

Together they entered the thick forest and began their hike south.

The Trail was a narrow path that wound around tall trees and short, stubby bushes. White blazes painted on rocks and trees marked the way. Sometimes the trail climbed straight up to mountaintops where they could see for miles and miles. Other times it cut right through towns where the white blazes were painted on sidewalks.

When the weather was good and the trail flat, Pam and Ellie could walk more then twenty miles a day. But in bad weather or over rough trail they might only make twelve miles a day. Wherever the white blazes led, Pam and Ellie would follow them all the way to Georgia.

*O*n such a long, difficult journey, Pam knew it was important to have a daily routine of hiking, eating, and resting.

But Ellie had her own routine. Every morning as Pam lay sleeping, Ellie snuck up and touched her cold, wet nose to Pam's nose.

"Oh!" Pam would cry as she jolted awake.

Ellie would smile as if to say,

"Gotcha!"

Then Pam would laugh and reply, "Good morning, Sunshine. Ready for a new day?"

Such a happy beginning to their days helped them face many challenges together.

*I*n October, as Pam and Ellie walked through Vermont, the weather was pleasant for many days in a row. Then, one evening just as they climbed into their tent, a huge storm blew in. Lightning flashed, thunder rolled, and wind shook their tent with every gust.

The storm raged for hours and hours. In the darkest part of the night, Pam and Ellie were startled by a loud *crack* followed by a terrifying explosion. It was a nearby tree crashing to the ground.

Crack! Another tree fell.

Crack! Crack! Crack!

All night long the wind blew down one tree after another. Pam was terrified. She was afraid one of the trees would smash them flat.

Ellie was scared, too. She crept up next to Pam. Pam wrapped her arm around the young dog and all through that long, terrible night they huddled together, comforting each other.

Finally, the storm ended at dawn. When they crawled out of the tent, Pam was shocked by what she saw.

The forest was now a tangle of fallen branches and toppled trees. Pam couldn't even find the trail.

But Ellie could. She could smell where other hikers had walked before the storm and she showed Pam the way.

*E*llie helped Pam in many ways, but sometimes Ellie needed Pam's help. Like once when they crossed a wide stream in Connecticut. Pam carried Ellie's pack so it wouldn't get wet.

Or when they came to a steep, rock wall, Pam helped by pushing Ellie up a series of ledges.

They also helped make each other happy, like when they played a game Ellie made up. Pam would take off her gloves during a break and Ellie would grab them and run off.

Ellie would play keep-away until Pam called, "Ellie! Drop it."

The game ended when she dropped the gloves and grinned at Pam with her doggie smile that said,

"Gotcha!"

Ellie's silliness always made Pam laugh. She liked having a fun partner on the Trail.

*I*n the mountains of Virginia, January brought snow. Ellie was excited to see big flakes falling from the sky and kept trying to snatch them out of the air.

But snow made the trail slick. On a steep hillside, Pam's feet flew out from under her. She tumbled down the slope.

"Aaaahhhhh!"

Pam screamed as she smashed into a tree.

Ellie raced to Pam's side. She sniffed Pam's head and whimpered.

Pam tried to stand up, but fell back in pain.

"Oh, Ellie," she cried, "my back is really hurt. I don't know if I can finish the hike."

With her paw, Ellie tapped Pam's shoulder as if to say, *"Please get up."*

Painfully, Pam struggled to her feet.

Ellie turned and walked a few steps down the trail then stopped and looked back at Pam. She wanted Pam to follow.

"Okay, I'll try." Pam limped up to Ellie.

Ellie moved a few more steps.

Again, Pam followed.

Together, they slowly inched down the trail.

The next day the weather turned bitterly cold. Pam's back was stiff and sore. She felt like giving up.

The trail was icy as Pam and Ellie hiked beside a cold, mountain stream. Down a ways, Pam could see that the stream turned into a waterfall. The stream and waterfall were almost completely frozen over.

Before Pam could stop her, Ellie was out on the ice sniffing around.

"Ellie, come here," Pam called softly trying to hide her fear.

But Ellie kept sniffing. The ice under her paws started to break.

"Ellie, come!" Pam yelled, panic taking over.

Crack! Splash!

Pam watched in horror as the ice gave way under Ellie and she plunged into the rushing water.

Ellie clawed at the edge of the ice with her front paws. She tried to pull herself out of the water but the ice broke again and again. She couldn't get out!

Pam tried to help but the ice was too thin. She couldn't reach Ellie.

Ellie was going to be swept under the ice and over the falls.

"Come on, Ellie!" Pam pleaded.

"Keep trying!"

Ellie's paws lost their grip. Her head began slipping beneath the surface. Ellie was going to drown!

"No!" Pam screamed. "Ellie, come!"

*E*llie heard Pam's command! She pushed her head back up to the surface. In one huge effort, she dug her toenails into the ice and heaved. This time the ice held. Ellie strained and strained with all her might until, *finally*, she got herself out of the water.

"Yes! Yes!" Pam shouted with joy.

Ellie shook herself off, looked at Pam as if to say,

"Come on, let's go"

and trotted down the trail as though nothing had happened.

Pam nodded. "You're right, Ellie. We have to keep going."

On the final day of their hike, after 199 days on the Trail, Pam and Ellie climbed down a long hill and walked onto a small parking lot. It was March and there were many hikers preparing to start on their own journeys.

"How far did you hike?" a man asked Pam. Other hikers stopped to look at the tired and dirty pair.

"Ellie and I hiked the entire Appalachian Trail," Pam said with a grin.

The crowd clapped and cheered. "Congratulations!" they shouted.

Ellie smiled and wagged her tail furiously.

"We did it, Ellie," Pam said, giving her a big hug. "We make a *very* fine team!"

Epilogue

On August 24, 2008, Pam and her dog, Ellie, left Baxter State Park in Maine to hike the Appalachian Trail. Their journey of more then 2,000 miles from Maine to Georgia took them just over six months. On March 10, 2009, after hiking all winter, Pam and Ellie arrived safely in Amicalola Falls State Park, Georgia. The two friends finished their journey in good health and high spirits.

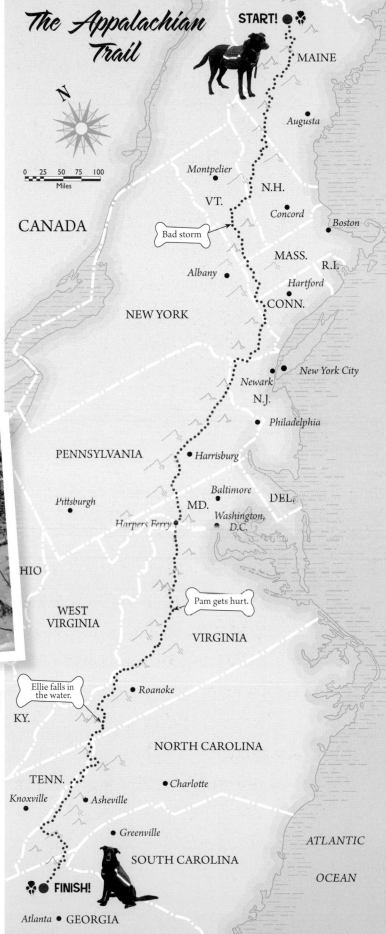

The Appalachian Trail

START!

MAINE

N

Augusta

0 25 50 75 100
Miles

Montpelier

N.H.

VT.

Concord

CANADA

Boston

Bad storm

MASS.

R.I.

Albany

Hartford

CONN.

NEW YORK

New York City

Newark

N.J.

Philadelphia

PENNSYLVANIA

Harrisburg

Baltimore

DEL.

Pittsburgh

MD.

Washington, D.C.

Harpers Ferry

HIO

Pam gets hurt.

WEST VIRGINIA

VIRGINIA

Ellie falls in the water.

Roanoke

KY.

NORTH CAROLINA

TENN.

Charlotte

Knoxville

Asheville

Greenville

ATLANTIC

SOUTH CAROLINA

OCEAN

FINISH!

Atlanta • GEORGIA

To my friend Kris Zuidema for her tireless work in making certain Ellie and I had all we needed on the Appalachian Trail. —P. F.

For Pam. —B. F.

Text © 2011 by Pam Flowers

Illustrations © 2011 by Bill Farnsworth

Published by A&A Johnston Press™

All rights reserved. No part of this book may be reproduced or transmitted in any form or by any means, electronic or mechanical, including photocopying, recording, or any information storage and retrieval system, without written permission from the publisher.

Library of Congress Control Number: 2010901102

ISBN (HB): 978-0-615-34076-0

ISBN (SB): 978-0-615-34077-7

Project editor: Michelle McCann

Managing editor: Kathy Howard

Production coordinator: Susan Dupèré

Designer: Elizabeth M. Watson

Mapmaker: Marge Mueller, Gray Mouse Graphics

To order books online visit: www.pamflowers.com

or call: 1-907-733-3307

Printed in China